PEACH
PERFECT

By
Sherri Eldridge

Illustrations by
Rob Groves

Peach Perfect

Published by:
Harvest Hill Press
Post Office Box 55
Salisbury Cove, Maine 04672
207-288-8900

ISBN: 1-886862-25-7

First printing: August 1998
Second printing: May 1999

PRINTED IN THE UNITED STATES
ON ACID-FREE PAPER

The recipes in this book were created with the goal of reducing fat, calories, cholesterol and sodium. They also present a variety of fresh healthy foods, to be prepared with love and eaten with pleasure.

CREDITS:

Cover border from cotton print gratefully used as a courtesy of:
Fabrics by Spiegel

Cover Design, Layout and Typesetting: Sherri Eldridge

Front Cover Watercolor and Text Line Art: Robert Groves

Text Typesetting and Proofreading: Bill Eldridge

PREFACE

The juicy scent and sweetness of the peach are reminders of the glory of summer. Peaches are great in desserts and fresh baking, but the best way to enjoy a peach is by simply eating it out of hand.

Peach trees grow in most temperate zones. Among deciduous (leaf-shedding) tree fruits, only the apple and pear are more widely distributed throughout the world than the peach.

Although the smooth skin and flavor of the nectarine suggests it is the cross of a peach and plum, it is in fact a peach variety.

There are two general categories of peaches - freestone and clingstone. A freestone peach is one in which the flesh readily parts from the pit. These are the primary eating varieties. The clingstone is a firmer, less juicy fruit and is more difficult to separate from the pit. These are used for canning as they can handle the heat of processing.

Cinnamon, nutmeg, ground coriander and mint are the spices that best bring out the flavor of peaches.

Peaches are loved for the flavor they bring to pies, ice cream, jams and muffins. And to a wintery day, last summer's canned peaches bring the glow of sunshine and the taste of freshness in every bite.

CONTENTS

Peach Pecan Pancakes

2 cups all-purpose flour
1 tablespoon baking powder
¼ teaspoon salt
1 egg
1 egg white
2 tablespoons sugar
1 tablespoon canola oil
2 cups skim milk
2 large peaches
¼ cup chopped pecans

Serving: 3 Pancakes
Protein: 9 gm
Carbs: 44 gm
Sodium: 360 mg

Calories: 274
Fat: 6.5 gm
Cholesterol: 37 mg
Calcium: 195 mg

SERVES 6

Sift together dry ingredients. In a separate bowl, beat eggs, then beat in sugar, oil and milk. Stir liquid mixture into dry ingredients.

Remove pits, and dice peaches into ¼-inch cubes. Gently fold peaches and pecans into batter.

Preheat griddle, then spray with non-stick oil. Ladle pancake batter onto griddle to make 4-inch-round pancakes. Cook till bubbles form, then flip to cook other side. Serve immediately with maple syrup or fruit sauce.

Poached Peach Omelette with Goat Cheese

SERVES 2

Filling:

2 fresh ripe peaches

½ cup blush wine

½ cup water

1 tablespoon sugar

2 teaspoons minced fresh
   mint

Omelette:

1 egg

3 egg whites

2 teaspoons water

1 teaspoon butter

1 oz. soft goat cheese

Garnish:

½ cup nonfat sour cream

Serving: 1/2 Recipe
Protein: 16 gm
Carbs: 29 gm
Sodium: 227 mg

Calories: 243
Fat: 6.5 gm
Cholesterol: 115 mg
Calcium: 122 mg

Wash peaches, remove pits, and cut each into 10 slices. In a saucepan, bring wine, water, sugar and mint to a boil. Lower heat and simmer 10 minutes. Add peach slices, simmer for 5 minutes. Remove saucepan from heat, cover pan and let peaches steep 15 minutes, or until tender. Remove peaches with slotted spoon. Discard any loose skins.

Whisk eggs with water. Heat omelette pan over high heat 1 minute, then melt ½ teaspoon butter in pan. Pour in half of the eggs. Tilt pan and push set eggs aside so omelette cooks quickly. When eggs are almost set, place half of cheese and a quarter of the peaches onto omelette. Fold in half and transfer to serving dish. Top with sour cream and another quarter of the peaches. Repeat process for second omelette.

Spiced Fruit Compote

If out of season, substitute canned fruit for fresh.

SERVES 8

1 pound peaches
1 pound apricots
1 pound pears
16 oz. can pineapple rounds
   in unsweetened juice
1 cup orange juice
¼ cup packed brown sugar
1 tablespoon lemon juice
1 3-inch cinnamon stick
4 whole cloves
pinch of ground mace

Serving: 1/8 Recipe
Protein: 2 gm
Carbs: 38 gm
Sodium: 4 mg

Calories: 153
Fat: 1 gm
Cholesterol: 0 mg
Calcium: 31 mg

Preheat oven to 350°. Spray 8" x 12" baking dish with nonstick oil.

Peel fruit and slice into rounds. Arrange sliced fruit and pineapple rounds in baking dish. Combine remaining ingredients in a saucepan and bring to a boil. Reduce heat, simmer 5 minutes, then remove cinnamon stick and cloves. Pour sauce over fruit.

Bake fruit for 30 minutes. Serve fresh and hot, or cover and chill spiced fruit for later use.

Peach Breakfast Custard

2 peaches
4 tablespoons brown sugar
½ cup nonfat plain yogurt
½ cup nonfat cottage cheese
½ cup skim milk
1 teaspoon vanilla extract
6 tablespoons sugar
¼ teaspoon cinnamon
1 egg
¼ teaspoon lemon juice
¼ cup flour

Serving: 1 Cup
Protein: 9 gm
Carbs: 49 gm
Sodium: 151 mg

Calories: 242
Fat: 1.5 gm
Cholesterol: 54 mg
Calcium: 134 mg

MAKES 4 CUSTARD CUPS

Preheat oven to 400°. Spray four 6-ounce custard cups with nonstick oil. Peel peaches and slice into thin crescents. Line custard cups with the peach slices, and sprinkle a tablespoon of brown sugar into each cup.

Put yogurt, cottage cheese and milk into blender and whip until very smooth. Add remaining ingredients and blend. Pour mixture in equal amounts over fruit in the custard cups.

Bake 30 minutes or until lightly golden on top. Loosen edges of custards with knife, invert cups onto plates and tap bottom of cup to loosen. Serve plain or with a fresh fruit sauce.

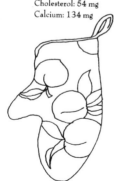

Peach Pecan Quick Bread

3 cups peeled and diced
   peaches
1 cup sugar
2 tablespoons canola oil
¼ cup packed brown sugar
1 egg
1 egg white
1 tablespoon lemon juice
3 cups all-purpose flour
½ cup chopped pecans
1 teaspoon baking soda
1½ tablespoons baking
   powder
1 teaspoon cinnamon
1 teaspoon nutmeg
1 cup lowfat buttermilk
¼ cup peach preserves

Serving: 1 Slice
Protein: 3 gm
Carbs: 28 gm
Sodium: 138 mg

Calories: 147
Fat: 3 gm
Cholesterol: 9 mg
Calcium: 43 mg

MAKES 2 LOAVES

Preheat oven to 350°. Spray two 9"x 5" bread pans with nonstick oil.

Put 1½ cups of the peaches into a bowl and sprinkle with ½ cup sugar. Put remaining peaches and sugar into blender and whip until smooth.

In large mixing bowl, beat oil, brown sugar, eggs and lemon juice, then add peach purée. In a separate bowl, combine dry ingredients. Alternately stir buttermilk and egg mixture into dry ingredients. Fold in diced peaches. Pour dough equally into bread pans. Bake 45 minutes, or until a toothpick inserted in center of each loaf comes out clean. Remove from oven and spread 2 tablespoons peach preserves on top of each bread loaf. Cool in pans for 10 minutes, then remove and cool on wire rack. Each bread makes 12 slices.

A Peachy History

The peach (*Prunus persica*) was once thought to have come from Persia, hence the "persica" in its name. Now it is believed that the peach originated in China, as it was mentioned in the writings of Confucius in the 5th century B.C. Peaches came to Europe over the Middle Eastern trade routes and via the Greek and Roman expeditions.

The Spanish explorers brought the fruit to the New World in the 16th century, and it found its way to Florida. Since peaches grow easily from seeds, the trees rapidly spread north and west. Upon their arrival in Virginia, English settlers found peaches growing wild throughout the area. Shortly after settling in Massachusetts in the early 18th century, an English governor ordered peach stones for planting in New England. By the close of the 1700s, peaches were planted throughout the colonies for home use. It was not until after the Civil War that commercial growing began (the main purpose of this commercial undertaking was to make peach brandy).

In 1870, commercial peach production was spurred on by the Elberta variety from the Marshallville, Georgia plantations. The Elberta has a large size, great beauty and excellent keeping qualities. By the late 19th century, both South Carolina and Georgia had extensive commercial orchards. Connecticut also had many peach orchards until the freeze of 1917 when the plantings were wiped out.

Peach Yogurt Muffins

1¼ cups all-purpose flour
1 cup rolled oats
¼ cup packed brown sugar
1 tablespoon baking powder
½ teaspoon baking soda
¼ teaspoon cinnamon
1 egg
1 egg white
1 cup plain nonfat yogurt
¼ cup honey
2 tablespoons canola oil
1 teaspoon vanilla extract
1 cup peeled and diced
   peaches

MAKES 12 MUFFINS

Preheat oven to 400°. Spray cups of muffin tin with nonstick oil.

Mix flour, oats, sugar, baking powder, baking soda and cinnamon together.

In a separate bowl, beat eggs, yogurt, honey, oil and vanilla until blended. Stir peaches into liquid mixture. Combine dry ingredients and liquid mixture with several quick strokes. Pour batter into 12 muffin cups. Bake 20 minutes, or until a toothpick inserted in center comes out clean. Cool muffins 5 minutes on a wire rack. Warm warm.

Serving: 1 Muffin
Protein: 4 gm
Carbs: 28 gm
Sodium: 179 mg

Calories: 159
Fat: 3 gm
Cholesterol: 18 mg
Calcium: 91 mg

Peach Slaw

2 cups peeled and diced
    peaches
1 tablespoon lemon juice
4 cups shredded cabbage
5 tablespoons sliced almonds
¼ cup raisins
¾ cup nonfat cottage cheese
¾ cup nonfat plain yogurt
¼ cup nonfat mayonnaise
2 tablespoons sugar
1 tablespoon white pepper
pinch of salt

SERVES 8

Sprinkle peaches with lemon juice. In a large bowl, combine cabbage, peaches, almonds and raisins.

To make dressing, place remaining ingredients in blender and process until smooth.

Mix dressing with cabbage mixture by repeatedly tossing. Cover slaw and chill at least 2 hours before serving.

Serving: 1/8 Recipe
Protein: 6 gm
Carbs: 19 gm
Sodium: 145 mg

Calories: 119
Fat: 3 gm
Cholesterol: 0 mg
Calcium: 91 mg

Peachy Keen Mint Mold

2 tablespoons gelatin
½ cup cold water
1½ cups peeled and sliced
    peaches
2 cups boiling water
¼ cup mint leaves
4 drops green food coloring
¾ cup sugar
3 tablespoons lemon juice

Serving: 1/6 Recipe
Protein: 3 gm
Carbs: 32 gm
Sodium: 5 mg

Calories: 136
Fat: 0 gm
Cholesterol: 0 mg
Calcium: 14 mg

SERVES 6

In a bowl, sprinkle gelatin over water.

Briefly poach peaches for 5 minutes in 2 cups of boiling water. Remove peaches with a slotted spoon, reserve hot liquid.

In a separate bowl, pour boiling peach liquid over mint leaves. Steep 10 minutes, then strain into gelatin. Mix in food coloring, sugar and lemon juice.

Rinse, but do not dry, the inside of a mold. Pour gelatin mixture into mold, chill. Just before it sets, arrange peach slices over gelatin. Chill overnight.

Peach Soup

½ cantaloupe
4 ripe peaches
¼ cup nonfat plain yogurt
¼ cup nonfat cottage cheese
2 tablespoons Grand
   Marnier or orange juice
2 tablespoons minced
   fresh mint

Serving: 1/4 Recipe
Protein: 4 gm
Carbs: 21 gm
Sodium: 65 mg

Calories: 111
Fat: 0.5 gm
Cholesterol: 0 mg
Calcium: 64 mg

SERVES 4

Cut ripe cantaloupe fruit away from rind. Peel peaches and remove pits.

Combine cantaloupe and peaches in a blender and whip until smooth. Add yogurt, cottage cheese and Grand Marnier and blend until smooth. Pour soup into bowls, stir in minced mint.

Cover and chill 3 hours before serving.

Peach Varieties and Production

The U.S. produces one-fourth of the world's peaches - 3 billion pounds each year. Half of the harvest goes into the fresh fruit market. Georgia, South Carolina, California, New Jersey and Pennsylvania are major producers of fresh peaches, as is Ontario, Canada. California mostly grows the clingstone peach varieties, which are canned, dried or frozen.

The peach harvesting season is May through September, with different varieties coming into season each month.

While there are literally hundreds of varieties, here are a few of the best. Desert Gold is a semifreestone, medium in size and firm even when ripe. It is one of the earliest peaches of the season. Sunhaven is a clingstone that is surprisingly juicy and sweet, good for eating and cooking, its season is in August. Redhaven is a freestone peach with plenty of flavor and juice, good for eating, cooking and preserving, its season is also in August. Fairhaven is a freestone peach, harvested in September, it is good both fresh and for baking. The Elberta peach is a freestone with lots of color, large, and juicy. This is the last peach of the season.

Peach Honey Baked Salmon

1½ lbs. fresh salmon fillets
5 peaches
3 tablespoons honey
1 tablespoon dry mustard
    (powder)
1 tablespoon lemon juice
1 teaspoon white pepper
1 teaspoon melted butter
½ teaspoon ground ginger
½ teaspoon finely grated
    lemon rind
2 tablespoons brown sugar

SERVES 4

Serving: 1/4 Recipe
Protein: 35 gm
Carbs: 34 gm
Sodium: 89 mg

Calories: 386
Fat: 12.5 gm
Cholesterol: 96 mg
Calcium: 48 mg

Prepare grill or preheat broiler. Spray aluminum foil with nonstick oil, then cover grill or broiler pan with foil. Remove any bones in fillets with pliers.

Peel peaches and cut into quarters. Dice enough to make ¼ cup and put into blender. Add honey, mustard, lemon juice, pepper and butter to blender and whip until sauce is smooth.

In a small bowl, mix ginger, grated lemon rind and brown sugar.

Arrange salmon fillets on grill or broiler with skin side up. Grill or broil 5 minutes, then turn fillets. Baste fillets with sauce. Arrange peach quarters around fillets, sprinkle spiced brown sugar mixture on peaches. Grill or broil another 5 minutes, until inner flesh is light pink. Spoon pan juices over fish.

Baked Stuffed Peaches

4 large fresh peaches
¼ cup blanched almonds
11-oz. can mandarin orange
    slices in water
1 tablespoon finely grated
    orange rind
¼ cup orange juice
½ cup powdered sugar
1 tablespoon lemon juice

Serving: 2 Peach Halves   Calories: 176
Protein: 2 gm   Fat: 3.5 gm
Carbs: 36 gm   Cholesterol: 0 mg
Sodium: 1 mg   Calcium: 35 mg

SERVES 4

Preheat oven to 350°. Spray baking dish with nonstick oil.

Peel peaches, cut in half and remove pits. Arrange peaches so that hollow faces up in baking dish.

Mince or grind almonds. Drain mandarin oranges.

In a small bowl, mix almonds, orange rind, orange juice and ¼ cup of the powdered sugar. Fill peach halves with mixture. Sprinkle filled peach halves with lemon juice, then sift remaining ¼ cup powdered sugar on top. Bake 10 minutes and serve immediately.

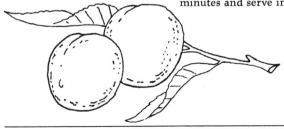

Dilled Peach Swordfish

2 teaspoons olive oil
1½ lbs. thick swordfish
    steaks (4 pieces)
1 teaspoon lemon juice
2 cups thinly sliced onions
2 teaspoons slivered garlic
1 teaspoon honey
1½ lbs. fresh peaches,
    peeled and diced
½ cup chopped fresh dill
1 lemon, cut into 4 wedges

Serving: 1/4 Recipe	Calories: 334
Protein: 36 gm	Fat: 8.5 gm
Carbs: 31 gm	Cholesterol: 66 mg
Sodium: 157 mg	Calcium: 53 mg

SERVES 4

Spray a large sauté pan with nonstick oil, then lightly coat with 1 teaspoon of olive oil. Remove skin from swordfish, sprinkle both sides with lemon juice, and place in pan.

Heat 1 teaspoon of olive oil in a small sauté pan, sauté onions and garlic until translucent. Reduce heat to medium and stir in honey. Cook 5 minutes. Stir in peaches and cook another 5 minutes. Add dill, then remove from heat.

Pan-fry swordfish on medium-high heat, just until flesh is opaque and firm to the touch. Spoon peaches around fish and heat 2 minutes. Transfer to serving plates, spooning peach sauce over fish. Serve immediately with lemon wedges.

Peach Pie

2¼ cups all-purpose flour
4 tablespoons sugar
pinch of salt
3 tablespoons canola oil
½ cup skim milk
2 tablespoons cornstarch
¼ cup apple juice
5 cups peeled peaches,
    pitted and sliced
1 tablespoon lemon juice
1 cup packed brown sugar
1 teaspoon almond extract
1 tablespoon butter
1 tablespoon skim milk
1 teaspoon cinnamon mixed
    with 1 tablespoon sugar

Serving: 1 Piece	Calories: 387
Protein: 5 gm	Fat: 7 gm
Carbs: 77 gm	Cholesterol: 4 mg
Sodium: 51 mg	Calcium: 60 mg

MAKES ONE 8-PIECE PIE

Preheat oven to 375°. Spray a 9-inch pie pan with nonstick oil.

Sift flour, sugar and salt together. In a separate bowl, combine oil and milk. Pour liquid into flour and blend with a fork. Wrap dough in plastic and chill 15 minutes. Divide dough in half. Roll each crust between sheets of wax paper. Place 1 crust in pie pan.

Dissolve cornstarch in apple juice, let rest 15 minutes. Mix peaches, lemon juice, brown sugar, almond extract and cornstarch mixture together. Pour peaches into pie crust, dot with butter and place top crust on pie. Pinch edges together, flute and trim. Make 5 slits in top crust, brush with milk and sprinkle with cinnamon and sugar. Bake 40 minutes, or until crust is light gold. Cool 30 minutes, serve warm or cold.

Peach Crumb Cobbler

6 packed cups peeled and
   sliced fresh peaches
½ cup sugar
1 tablespoon lemon juice
1 teaspoon finely chopped
   fresh mint
3 tablespoons cornstarch
2 tablespoons orange juice
½ cup all-purpose flour
½ cup packed light brown
   sugar
2 teaspoons cinnamon
2 tablespoons butter

Serving: 1/9 Recipe
Protein: 2 gm
Carbs: 44 gm
Sodium: 33 mg

Calories: 201
Fat: 3 gm
Cholesterol: 7 mg
Calcium: 28 mg

SERVES 9

Preheat oven to 350°. Spray a 9-inch square deep-dish pie plate with nonstick oil.

In a mixing bowl, combine peaches, sugar, lemon juice and mint. Mix cornstarch and orange juice, let rest 15 minutes, then mix into peaches. Pour peach mixture into prepared pie plate.

Mix flour with brown sugar and cinnamon. Use a pastry cutter to cut butter into flour until mixture resembles coarse crumbs. Sprinkle over peaches. Bake 45 minutes. Serve hot.

Peach Upside-Down Cake

¼ cup packed light brown sugar

2 cups peeled and sliced fresh peaches

1 teaspoon nutmeg

1 cup all-purpose flour

¾ cup sugar

2 teaspoons baking powder

¼ teaspoon baking soda

1 teaspoon cinnamon

pinch of salt

2 tablespoons soft butter

½ cup lowfat buttermilk

1 teaspoon vanilla extract

Serving: 1/12 Recipe
Protein: 2 gm
Carbs: 30 gm
Sodium: 128 mg

Calories: 139
Fat: 2 gm
Cholesterol: 5 mg
Calcium: 40 mg

SERVES 12

Preheat oven to 350°. Spray an 8-inch cake pan with nonstick oil.

Sprinkle bottom of pan with brown sugar. Arrange the peach slices on bottom of pan in a tight pinwheel. Sprinkle with nutmeg and set aside.

In a mixing bowl, sift together flour, sugar, baking powder, baking soda, cinnamon and salt. Beat butter, buttermilk and vanilla into flour until smooth. Gently pour batter over peaches. Bake 45 minutes, or until a toothpick inserted in cake comes out clean. Cool 10 minutes, then gently turn out onto platter.

Selecting and Storing Peaches

The perfect peach is ripe and firm, but not hard. Smell the fruit for that sweet fresh "peachy" aroma. Fragrance is a good indicator of ripeness. The color should be creamy to gold with no sign of green. (Peaches picked green will never ripen, they only soften and gain nothing in flavor.) The red color in peaches is not a sign of ripeness, only of the variety. Avoid peaches with bruising or brown spots, which betray a stage of decay.

Peaches do not sweeten after they have been harvested, and cold storage will give them a woolly texture. This is a good reason to find locally grown, tree-ripened peaches - they will be the best.

Peaches are harvested ripe and firm for shipment to market. They will complete ripening in two to three days in a ripening bowl, or in a bag kept out of direct sunlight. If using a paper bag, make sure it has air holes. Once ripe, wrap in plastic and store in the refrigerator.

Peaches have no sodium, cholesterol or fat. They are a source of ascorbic acid, niacin, vitamin A, potassium and fiber. Much of the flavor and nutrients are stored in the peach skin. When a peeled peach is needed for baking, cover with boiling water, let stand one minute, and the skin will easily strip off. Discard the pit, as the almond-like kernel in it is high in deadly prussic acid.

Creamy Peach Freeze

2 cups peeled and diced
    peaches, juice reserved
2 tablespoons crystallized
    ginger
2 tablespoons lemon juice
½ cup nonfat plain yogurt
½ cup nonfat cottage cheese
1 teaspoon plain gelatin
¼ cup cold water
¼ cup peach juice
½ cup sugar
1 egg white at room
    temperature

Serving: 1/4 Recipe	Calories: 210
Protein: 8 gm	Fat: 0 gm
Carbs: 47 gm	Cholesterol: 0 mg
Sodium: 135 mg	Calcium: 95 mg

SERVES 4

Place peaches and reserved juice, ginger and lemon juice in food processor or blender and process until puréed. Add yogurt and cottage cheese, whip until completely smooth.

Combine gelatin and water in saucepan and let rest for 15 minutes. Over low heat, warm gelatin mixture with ¼ cup peach juice and ⅓ cup of the sugar. Stir until sugar dissolves. Remove from heat and whisk mixture 4 minutes. Whisk puréed mixture into gelatin. Put into the freezer for 30 minutes, removing every 10 minutes to whisk.

In a separate bowl, beat egg white into soft peaks. Continue beating while adding remaining sugar until stiff. Fold egg white into peach mixture. Transfer to serving bowls, cover and refrigerate at least 8 hours before serving.

Peaches Flambé

1 tablespoon butter
3 tablespoons brown sugar
4 peeled and sliced
    fresh peaches
2 ripe bananas
3 oz. brandy or dark rum
1 tablespoon sugar

Optional: Nonfat vanilla
    frozen yogurt

Serving: 1/4 Recipe	Calories: 219
Protein: 1 gm	Fat: 3.5 gm
Carbs: 36 gm	Cholesterol: 8 mg
Sodium: 36 mg	Calcium: 17 mg

SERVES 4

In a large skillet, melt butter over low heat. Add brown sugar and stir until dissolved. Add peach slices and cover. Stir occasionally until peaches start to juice up. Peel and cut bananas into lengthwise quarters, then into 2-inch strips. Increase heat to medium-high and when peaches are tender, add bananas. Cook 2 minutes longer, then cover and remove from heat.

In separate saucepan, heat liquor for 4 minutes over low heat . Place fruit in flambé dish, sprinkle with sugar and pour warm liquor over all. Cover for 1 minute, remove cover, stand back and light! Serve flambé when flame goes out, preferably over frozen yogurt.

Peach Melba

4 fresh peeled peaches,
   pitted and cut in half,
   with skins reserved
2 cups white dry wine
1 cinnamon stick
4 whole cloves
2 cups honey
½ cup currant jelly
1 cup sieved raspberries
1 teaspoon cornstarch
½ cup sugar
4 sprigs fresh mint

Serving: 1/4 Recipe
Protein: 1 gm
Carbs: 73 gm
Sodium: 15 mg

Calories: 285
Fat: 0.5 gm
Cholesterol: 0 mg
Calcium: 20 mg

SERVES 4

In a large saucepan, boil peach skins, wine, cinnamon, cloves and honey for 5 minutes. Strain liquid and return it to saucepan. Bring to a boil, add peach halves. Remove from heat, and allow liquid and peaches to cool.

In the top pan of a double boiler over boiling water, bring jelly and raspberries to a boil. Remove a few tablespoons of the liquid, cool 5 minutes, then whisk cornstarch and sugar into cooled liquid. Stir back into boiling raspberry mixutre, and cook until sauce is thick and clear. Chill for 3 hours.

Using a slotted spoon, remove peaches from poaching liquid and place 2 halves in each of 4 dessert dishes. Spoon raspberry sauce over peaches, garnish with fresh mint.

Peach Sorbet

4 cups peeled and diced
   fresh peaches, and their
   juice
¾ cup fresh lemon juice
1 cup sugar
5 tablespoons Amaretto
   liqueur or orange juice
   concentrate

Serving: 1/8 Recipe   Calories: 169
Protein: 1 gm   Fat: 0 gm
Carbs: 40 gm   Cholesterol: 0 mg
Sodium: 1 mg   Calcium: 6 mg

SERVES 8

In a blender, whip peaches and their juice until smooth.

Heat remaining ingredients in a saucepan over low heat until sugar is dissolved. Remove from heat and stir in peach purée.

Pour into an 8-inch square pan and set in freezer. Using a rubber spatula, stir every 15 minutes until creamy, about 2 hours. Cover and allow to freeze. To serve, scoop into small dishes and garnish with fresh fruit.

Brandied Peach Preserves

4 lbs. fresh peaches
2 cups sugar
3 cups water
½ cup brandy

Serving: 1/4 Cup
Protein: 0 gm
Carbs: 19 gm
Sodium: 1 mg

Calories: 81
Fat: 0 gm
Cholesterol: 0 mg
Calcium: 3 mg

MAKES 2 QUARTS

Rub fuzz off peaches with a coarse towel. Rinse, halve and pit peaches. Combine sugar and water in a large pot and cook into a syrup. Add peaches, simmer 10 minutes. Remove peaches with a slotted spoon and place in 4 sterilized canning jars. Pour 2 tablespoons brandy over peaches in each jar, then fill jars to within ½ inch of top with hot syrup. Seal jar according to manufacturer's directions.

Place jars on rack in boiler half-filled with boiling water, leaving space between jars. Add boiling water to cover jars 2 inches above their tops. Bring to boil, cover, and process 15 minutes. Using tongs, lift out jars (not by their lids) and set on towels with several inches between them to cool.

Peach Chutney

MAKES 2 QUARTS

1 cinnamon stick
10 whole cloves
¼ teaspoon coriander seeds
cheesecloth and string
2 cups sugar
1¼ cups cider vinegar
10 fresh peeled and diced
    peaches
1 tablespoon preserved
    ginger, finely chopped
¼ cup chopped citron or
    orange peel
2 tablespoons candied
    lemon peel

Serving: 2 Tablespoons   Calories: 33
Protein: 0 gm   Fat: 0 gm
Carbs: 9 gm   Cholesterol: 0 mg
Sodium: 0 mg   Calcium: 2 mg

Tie cinnamon, cloves and coriander in a piece of cheesecloth. Bring sugar and vinegar a to boil over medium heat. While boiling, add spice bag and all other ingredients. Simmer 10 minutes, then remove spice bag. Remove fruit pieces with a slotted spoon and place in 4 sterilized canning jars. Fill each jar to within ½ inch of top with hot syrup. Seal jars according to manufacturer's directions.

Place jars on rack in boiler half-filled with boiling water, leaving space between jars. Add boiling water to cover jars 2 inches above their tops. Bring to boil, cover, and process 15 minutes. Using tongs, lift out jars (not by their lids) and set on towels with several inches between them to cool.

Peach Cooler

1 cup chopped peeled
   peaches
1 cup skim milk
4 tablespoons honey
¼ teaspoon almond extract
8 - 10 cracked ice cubes
2 sprigs fresh mint

Purée peaches in blender. Add milk, honey and almond extract and process until smooth. With blender running at high speed, add ice cubes 1 at a time and process until smooth.

Pour thick shakes into 2 tall glasses and serve with a sprig of mint.

Serving: 1/2 Recipe
Protein: 5 gm
Carbs: 50 gm
Sodium: 72 mg

Calories: 217
Fat: 0.5 gm
Cholesterol: 2 mg
Calcium: 166 mg

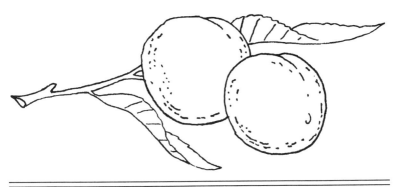